body works

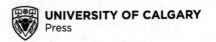
UNIVERSITY OF CALGARY
Press

body works

dennis cooley

Brave & Brilliant Series
ISSN 2371-7238 (Print) ISSN 2371-7246 (Online)

University of Calgary Press
2500 University Drive NW
Calgary, Alberta
Canada T2N 1N4
press.ucalgary.ca

LIBRARY AND ARCHIVES CANADA CATALOGUING IN PUBLICATION

Title: Body works / Dennis Cooley.
Names: Cooley, Dennis, 1944- author.
Series: Brave & brilliant series ; no. 30.
Description: Series statement: Brave & brilliant series, 2371-7238 ; no. 30 | Poems.
Identifiers: Canadiana (print) 20220494665 | Canadiana (ebook) 2022049469X | ISBN
    9781773854489 (hardcover) | ISBN 9781773854496 (softcover) | ISBN 9781773854502 (PDF)
    | ISBN 9781773854519 (EPUB)
Classification: LCC PS8555.O575 B63 2023 | DDC C811/.54—dc23

The University of Calgary Press acknowledges the support of the Government of Alberta
through the Alberta Media Fund for our publications. We acknowledge the financial support
of the Government of Canada. We acknowledge the financial support of the Canada Council
for the Arts for our publishing program.

Printed and bound in Canada by Marquis
This book is printed on 55 Enviro Book Natural paper

Editing by Helen Hajnoczky
Cover photo by Alexander Grey on Unsplash
Cover design, page design, and typesetting by Melina Cusano

In memory of Birk Sproxton

Contents

for the time being | 1

beached | 3
seismic | 4
Cinderella | 5
for the time being | 6
memes | 7
the clocks we lock | 8
the body, drowning | 9
out of time | 10
winter coming down | 11
the runner | 12
the watch tower | 13
time's up | 16
travelling light | 17
blown away | 18
so long | 19
about time | 20
right on time | 21
to speak in place of | 22
time and wind | 23
right here dear reader | 24
when you are you | 25
it's time, its time | 26

disjointed | 27

regret | 28
it was the height | 29
to calculate if it is not | 32
quite the you | 33
by & by | 34
the foot | 35
xoxoxoxox | 38
think of me | 39
saint alm ost | 41
she pulls up lame | 42
the times are out of joint | 44
the tug & yawk | 45
you could hear | 46
where we unravel | 47
bone house | 48

the body abroad | 49

the body arrives | 50
body works | 52
celestial coordinates | 54
annunciation | 55
but the body | 58
the relique | 59
Ulysses returns | 61
Gijon | 63
Le Pétomane | 64
the chapel of bones | 66
the young in Coimbra | 68
a disquisition on beauty | 69
the inner ear | 70

the body politic | 71

salt | 72
across the line | 74
immunity | 76
Julio Portillo's body | 78
newsreel | 79
pope orders priests to quit politics | 80
penny wise | 82
BJ: a tie game | 84

body works | 87

the winter of their discontent | 88
Fort-Da | 89
lost at sea | 90
woman in love | 91
let there be light | 92
the angels arrive | 94
the latest edition | 96
ex libris | 97
beribboned | 98
listen | 100
the idea of order at due north | 101
body parts | 102
as the spirit moves us | 106
for that matter | 108
anatomy of melancholy | 110
at night Cooley listens | 111
their startling beauty | 114
to be in | 115
supplicant | 116
the machinery of his breathing | 117
they find their tongues | 118
quite the whopper | 119

first thing you know | 120
the best that is said | 122
back gammon | 124
the fact of the matter | 125
summer dream | 126

the heart of the matter | 129

spiffy | 130
you and your dried-pea heart | 131
overtaken | 132
your heart exposed | 134
mayhems of the heart | 135
to give a little | 136
help for the lovelorn | 137
ms. lonelyhearts | 139
his heart, awry | 140
he returns | 143
heartless | 144
perturbations of the heart | 145
an "H" in the heart | 146

for the time being

beached

salt wind & the gulls
,thick,
thick,
the tides
wishing,, wishing,, wishing

the surge & wash of kids
until the surf drains
in a heavy sucking sound
and the world is sinking

in yr hourglass heart
the sun burning
the rub of sand
slowly moving

the beach is stinking
with mud & small creatures
dying in their mucous

kelp drying & the stench of fish
the wharves bedraggled
in broken shells   plastic pails
lost sandals   matted towels

the wharves bedraggled
the wind stinging
an old man talking
to himself and digging
in the sand

seismic

if where we wait in our lives we felt
the allure of where they might have gone,
places we fear to go or hope to land,
someone else we could have been—

when we feel, in the earth,
a small shiver we never knew—
we knew or would recognize
perhaps a god who (says s/he) loves us—

a filament that burns on the cloudiest day,
and with a small warm light—

the beautiful heartache we always wanted.

Cinderella

every year
      some thing
same thing
      some one

swimming among
      clinkers,

            something rescinded—

what is thatched & cached,
what tethered & feathered,
in drift and in tumour caught,
and in time delivered.

rumours of what is to come,
as lethal as gossip, as malicious
as the murmurings
          in our glass hearts

for the time being

they blunder into us and
they make us their own
particulars their known familiars
perilously unaffiliated
and in no way benign

> win us over fooling
> us into believing
> once upon a time
> we were the one
> and only one

they will have their way
they will always leave
they want to break up
run off with something or other
disassemblingly making up
another story, pure alchemy

> being unconscionably fickle
> they're off for some bit
> of fluff that's not us & that's it
> /that's it for us
> we are history we
> are goners our hopes of sticking
> together dashed
> the whole affair completely mortifying

> they have their fun,
> their little fling, they have
> their way with us,
> our rank and trembling desires

memes

where's the harm
in the end we will

Drown in yellow
Memes & Mem
ories our cries
Bright orioles

Ever & Anon
Ymous as an
Emones drawn in

One an other
'S charms
Crying out
Like love
Rs or ene
Mies

the clocks we lock

and choke in
the bones click and lock

time stumbles
inside the stomach
tobacco darkens
the ribs, all the way up the stairway.

the room booms and bangs,
the door slams shut
rattles the kitchen.

the room breathes hard,
grampa's cough passes
through the oil-slow darkness,

grampa's fingerbones cast their chalk
against the wall
all night long they
shake into the hallway

the shadows hang onto the wall
the air strains with listening

the body, drowning

our arms wide
eyes open as birds
so also our warthog hearts

wash up in ropey tangles
in gurgles up our throats
our waterlogged worries

they come on tumble and coil
and we hold cold

feet against our hearts
to keep us warm

hold court in
the armory of the seas

our small bones
going under

out of time

to be for ever running out of time
  be for ever running out of time to
    for ever running out of time to be
      ever running out of time to be for
        running out of time to be for ever
          out of time to be for ever running
            of time to be for ever running out
              time to be for ever running out of

winter coming down

summer tumbles
down the neighbour's wall
hangs in the virginia creeper
like sleeping bats

a softness we can breathe
till it fits like moleskin

teaches us to lie down
where animals run
blind & crying

before the back yard
fills up with cold

all dark long refuses

to touch
the body
its small
dark fuses

the runner

reconsiders the similes
            of mobility
                        the limits
            of mortality

knows the grass is
perennial, that in a
twitch of fire we
are gone like smoke—

that god shakes
at his ear a giant time

piece, by whose pace
we live & die.

knows what inside
the dog's pink ears
& our own ink
has gone
missing, what it is
to have lost track,
& no longer able
to keep it.

time & time
we are out of time—

            leaving it
                        all behind

the watch tower

Horology they call it,
the time-keeping. The hoarding of time.

John Scott, twice a year, fall and spring,
ticking off our mortal days,
attends the hours. His time is up and he
climbs the stairs half-way to heaven
where he can adjust the carillon
that runs the bells and chimes
that tell the time.

When he scans the massive wheels and cogs,
he may think of Newton who discerned
the fixing of stars and planets.

John Scott ascends because he can thank
those who came before him
"for good genes" and for the ability
to hold up time high in the city's towers,
where they thwack off the days and years.
Like coins in the Royal Canadian Mint.

John Scott, strange saboteur,
puts a wrench in the works,
puts a hand to them, a stop to time.
Halts time where it dangles around him.
The world freed
in march to light,
to slumber in fall,

as the gorgeous Prague clock in blue and green
which since 1410 has measured out
time immemorial ancient time and street time
sunrise daybreak star time twilight glowing

in numbers and letters and beautiful gold parabolas
since Ezekiel beheld wheels in wheels in wheels arolling,
and the clock's fabled first creator was blinded, some said,
        that none should make another.

John Scott, akin to jewelers and watchmakers,
knows his work must be done, alone,
no wasting time in a far and distant tower
among the winds and pigeons.

Way above the little people in the street
he cannot turn his back to
he will turn back time
and time again know he cannot
reverse the imperturbable machine
that inside him too revolves.

Still he is the watch man and he
climbs into the clock and he
touches it gently   with his hands.

He knows his days among the pigeons
are numbered and though he has
the hang of it he can save only so much
light when he hoists himself
into the giant heart he can almost
feel it alive; it soothes him. The tick-tock
of the clock gets him, he says.
He can feel it all the time, inside.

He knows he cannot save himself.

A professor at UBC says, yes,
they are remarkable, the clocks. The
clock master too, who surprises the music,
assures it always will be on time.

Too bad, the professor says,
horology has fallen behind the times.
Too bad it's a dying art.

time's up

its time is done,
& from time to time,
               yours is too—
right on time, it would seem,
you got off on the wrong foot.

time to be stepping
in, putting a stop to

you could quit killing
time, though you have a lot
on your hands,
& there is no end,
no mend to forever—
few amends for anything.

talking and trying
        to wash
your hands of
trying to keep it
or keep up with it

beyond measure—
it is time you knew
it is time to be
up and at it—
no time to lose.

travelling light

reaching out to touch his wife—
she wasn't

there—the time he yanked
through his sleeve
the scarf that he dropped
on the way back—

the bodies we hold
in casual delinquency,
as a matter of light occupancy,

as if time
did not go
all the way through—

as if we were not
fireflies in a jar—
or the breath of gravity

blown away

who among us does not
want to lead our lives
        in delight, believe we are
        blown into radiance
        as if from the mouth of god,
        as if shining bubbles
        from the hand of a child

who does not know
we thrash on winds
that shadow us
whose light & dark
poke into us—

that, sometimes, abiding,
        we are blown
                off to the side
                out of the way—

        and one time—
        never come back.

so long

water soaks
the earth
the world—
an hour
glass we can
not see
our selves

in—for long,
so long,
my uncle fall
ing through

water, through paper,
so long lives this

so long, the young man
standing at the door said,
he was

    out of time
    off to war

    so long, he said
    so long, I'll be
      seeing you

about time

thought for some
time when i am

dead you will be a little
lonely yet you will not

miss me much
you will not much

miss me
still i like

to think you will
when the cat

wants in or out
think of me

when he does
when you do

> let him
> in or
> out you
> should
> know it

> is a
> bout time
> i was
> thinking

right on time

you better believe,
though you prick like a nettle with complaint,

yet will the plants thrive with the ants
yet will ants seek sweetness among the peonies

though down on your knees you sequester your thoughts
in a bowl of pennies, a jar of buttons, a ball of twine,
the planets will more or less in time
align, and on time arrive

even if you yourself will have
deadheaded the marigolds and pinched
all hopes from the beans, even if you
detained the cold at your ankles
until the moon feels frost-bitten

it will start when march
shows up in a mudpack
and high as a soprano sings

to speak in place of

the sliding bet
ween you & me
& who is even speaking

you & i & I & you
we two, we too are prone
to change with pronounced ten
dencies st rangely shifting

we do not know
who is who & who
is not

how can we
know, other
wise see
eye to eye,
or say any thing

i does not be
come you

in the end
it may be held again
st me—

how unbecoming,
you will say,
what are we
coming to

time and wind

all time and wind go for ever our lives over
time and wind go ever for our lives over all
and wind ever go for our lives time all over
ever wind go for our lives all time over and
go for our ever lives over all time and wind
for our lives over ever and all time wind go
our lives and wind go ever for over all time

right here dear reader

one billion atoms alone have escaped
    the page you now are
        /looking at

     right here
      dear reader

               here
       or here
         here is your chance—

all these atoms (will) pry loose and take up
residence in your own windy body

             as if in ceremony
             as if in loving you

when you are you

who is to know how
it goes with any of us

or when & why
or where it is now

& who you are
when you are there

or why you are who
or where you are

when you say you are

it's time, its time

we're done you say,
from time to time

its time is up
its time has come

and gone and
yours too, it's time
you were stepping

in for a change, put
a stop to this

you haven't a lot left

let this be on your two
-timing hands & tongue

there can be no end to forever—
talking and all the—
wishing and wringing
and washing your hands of

your time is up
it's time, you say

time to be up and at it
time to call it a day

disjointed

regret

You are going to
regret this.
She said.
Peremptorily, he thought.

He had hoped merely
to set sail
in sparkling regatta speak
the honied words
feel the zephyrs
wafting across the waters
far and compelling

as a whale's song
in what she said

She said:
1. may your neck bones grind with grit.
2. may your two hips fill with grout.
3. your two shoulders grate and crumble to bread.
4. may your one back harden to porcelain.
5. gout would be too good for you.
6. you and your stolen measures.

She gripped,
Onto his leg.
Beset his days.
Reset his gait.

With halting.

Measures.

it was the height

                              of every thing surely
                              things were looking
                              up—the very zenith
so light was the morning
he felt a spring in his step

i.
the morning in solicitude
the birds in their sweetness steeping
the sweepstakes of living
slipped out of the vertigo
they called spring, how comely
she in the back hoicking colours
prod i gaily out of the ground

the ladder was half way to heaven
the world veering open

        he thought it was
the very steps of comedy
he stood upon and felt
a tingle in his body
the hurry of things in the air

                              he was putting up
                              with nothing, he was
                              putting up bookshelves,
                              and they would flood
                              the room with music

ii.
his a bold & visionary move
              the professor—
                        \no hesitation   \
              setting up

a splendiferous place where
a barrage of sunlight arrived
and brightened the glass
splashed in wax & the smell of grass

iii.
he could merely have fallen
         in a light shower
                   when he lost
         his balance &   top
                              pled
    if he had known to watch
his step when the world is jogging past

               it is then
      he falls

         wham

         onto the cement

rams his ankle, shin, knee
he ups & breaks his hip

                        how unseemly how un
                          be coming falling
                               down he is
                             getting behind

further & further
in arrears, having lost
his every dignity.

iv
had thought to end up
standing on his own
two feet & an occasional iamb

i am, he said, therefore i rhyme.
ergo i go, eager as a
long-ago iamb to the laughter
he would not take it
lying down.

v.
so shaken was he when
it dawned on him
he would take the fall for it
poet in name only he would be
by the muses forsaken & forever move
in slow and drastic measures.

to calculate if it is not

      1. too late

      2. to tutor one's bones

      3. to mind one's tongue

      4. what it is

      5. to articulate

- to connect by using a joint between the parts
- to form a joint
- to enunciate distinct and precise sounds
- to separate into jointed segments
- to position or reposition
- to make intelligible
- to give clarity to
- to speak fluently and coherently, uninterruptedly, without pause or digression
- to show a facility with words
- to utter clearly in distinct syllables
- to be capable of speech
- to make sounds with the body's organs

                    - and so to enjoin
                    - one to another
                    - to join in signing
                    - to sing with
                    - the heart's tongue

quite the you

quite the me
thod, the art
hritic shoulders

the thud of door—
      one big shudder
      one bent shoulder

drags the week in & out,
the ends bedraggled

he is a carpet hung from winter
    whack whack
an old woman knocking
the cold off course

            of course we rehearse
      our methods and lists of hers & his
    trionics as they involve

    the bones in a wrist
    that spin & threaten
          to pop

by & by

lightning on the edge of the world,
a screen upon which shapes fling—

    gifts of the moment
        wrapt in tissue—

the days burn & shiver
nights chill & fever

          the earth on a string,
          we spinmaking
          bone assuming camouflage
          the film of flesh to hide
          the bones we strike to make
          our music.

    prepare for the day we will be
    joined in a sigh, side by side
        and in quiet rooms lie
        thigh by thigh

        bye bye bye
        good bye

                    in the suite—
          by & by

the foot

What it is to get off on a good footing:

tibia:
> a pipe, a flute, a wind instrument; to tip a tibia, a pipe
> line to, a pipe dream, a long long way to Tipperary, a
> bone dance, abundance

fibula:
> a pin, a skewer, the long thin bone of the leg, a fib, a
> fabulous helper and a support in hard times, a bow to
> play the tibia

tarsus:
> a wicker frame, a wicker basket, a wicked wicket, a
> basket case, do not go to hell in

metatarsus:
> beyond the tarsus, long past, a long time waiting

talus:
> a dice, a square bone, queer bone, square dance, time
> for a little shaking a bit of throwing, you rolls the bones
> and takes your chances, the vice is cast, you come up
> snake eyes, no dice s/he said, enough (of) dicing and
> slicing, time for deciding

calcaneus:
> the heel, the cad, do not trust the heel, heel to no one,
> we kick up, a time to jounce, heel toe & away we go, heel
> fellow well met, time to hail, a time to heal a ruptured
> tendon

navicular:
> a small boat, floating on water waltzing on air, a light
> dancer, light on our feet, to feel light in our feet, the
> light foot hears you, vehicular with pneuma, water
> music, the light in our face

35

cuboid:

> to be even-sided, even-tempered, sweet of nature, even
> so, cuboid pull back your beau

cuneiform:

> with which we take firm measures, put our foot down,
> or into, stepping in where we may, as we may cutting in
> on a partner, making a point, our songs written in clay
> (or water)

phalanx:

> yes, as you feared, dear reader, things get worse.
> disconcerting. the martial drums, the row of soldiers,
> bones in a row, get them in place, foot soldiers, Roman,
> in close formation, and their name shall be legion, they
> are on their toes, to Pretoria, marching as to war, a
> breaking of the peace, keeping pace, better step aside,
> (and who then in the vanguard, who Uriah dead in
> battle? who hip, ahead of the times most of the time,
> fractious?), which, proximal or distal, when we tip-toe
> the light fantastic

sesamoid:

> the tiny bone the size of a seed. seed bone, sesame. oh
> pen sense me. selfsame. same to me, she to you, seize
> the day

digitus:

> we dig it thus: we give the finger, toe the line, stub our
> toe, thumb the nose, knuckle under, stand on, point
> with, keep our balance, show the way, strain bruise
> crack embrace, digitalis for the broken heart

hallux:

> the hulking toe, great toe, Big Toe, Big Hunk. Hunky-
> dory. Outta the way. Punk Digit. Heads the dance,
> big lug, shows the way, home base, seldom swayed or
> snubbed or turned away, will never toe the line, even
> when we stub it. Except for gout, gout's its Achilles Heel.

dorsum:

        the back of the foot which is to say the top of the foot;
        with which we dance back to back, front to back, back
        to front, and, most blessedly, front to front, two by two
        by two by two, cheek by cheek, we too, we keep afloat,
        no cause for affront

plantar:

        upon which we stand, on our own two feet, on
        principle, on ceremony, a platter, from which we derive
        grace and balance, on which we right ourselves, pitter
        patter learn to keep our feet, to save our souls, to feel
        the fasciitis, the facts of the matter, warts and all

XOXOXOXOX

sprinklers jet the air
   with X's and O's
      their bright sign
         natures of love

      our bones steep in sun
thoughts wet with weeds

let us be then
              X static

we could behave
      with the decency of
         dogs at a bone

hopeful as gamblers
      our pockets full of wind

think of me

                    as a screen
              door we dangle
like caterpillars from the thread
        -ends of the calendar

                    and the new sun—
              slightly brighter than
              a brand-new dime—
              looks much unlike
              the lamp upon which
              moths alight in the dust
              & in stillness bump.

    the world trundles by
    the shelves we store
    our lives like spiders on

    the hinges squeak when i arrive
    and your smile slaps shut

    flies in their excitement
    where you pass through
    the kitchen peanut
    butter glued to the counter

    the room where the bath
            towel hangs
    another in which pillows lay
    faces wide open & shining

    when i leave sucking my knuckles
    you fling the screen
    door open / swat it shut
                    bam\\\

/that's me
or is it you
            closing
up behind

saint alm ost

born to sharpen bones
in ossuarial love
to whittle light from heaven
that will stain our sleep

and you   ) your loneliness
a long side the moon
where it pools by the windows

faith in the body's nakedness
its loveliness

between moon & sun conduct
the warm traffic of blood
bits of night orbit
the lunate in your wrist
small satellite around which
day & night seven bones
bunch like frost

she pulls up lame

meanwhile the wind is eating
the same sun that smelled
the buffalo that breathed
great hairy coughs of air

where she runs the air is forked
and filled with misgivings

that's me she says
catching a glimpse
'ts me all right
on the limp but

phlegmatic as all getout
that & dropdead
gorgeous, that's me,
gold lamé, the works,
wrapped in bright
garments of flesh

riding the meniscus
the crescent moon
that eases the knee
and disperses the weight

it's about time,
i shall say, it's me,
me and my gouty feet,

you haven't a ghost
of a chance she will say
who would have guessed but

it's you all right
it's you, old goat,
you and your knubby bones
me & my bloodred shoes

the times are out of joint

how right it is
a real revelation—
dealing with art
hritis, fit & mete is it
tho the metre's kaput &
the joints don't meet

in the noisy air & in
terstices the years im
pale the flesh
at times the times
are out of
joint.

O cur said,
spite our sad fat
her who art
right is hollow
wed wld be thy game
      the whole creat
      ion the hole
      crate & ka boo
      dull—failing.

his best cal
culations his very
elations all his ululations
falling ap art in stut
ter ring and in art
i culati
on

the tug & yawk

three sheets to the wind
the creak in the rig
    ging the free
       queynt stops
pages stop & ring

         signs every
where hollering halt halt
       who goes

there who dare air
those who care
to breathe the air

gauge the body's langu
age at the bottom of a mine
in acrid and canaried fumes
the spasms carried to
the heart before the vert

ebrae snap
O pen & shut O
pen ning & clo
sing up & down
the brae for
ever & a non
     in & out
up & down the line

you could hear

                    the chain jerk
                    through the links

the torque in the chin, the fatigue,
the sharp pique in the marrow
the tongue a broken hinge to tomorrow

        fell into a fit
        of gout a bout
        ten years ago
        a bit tame but
        a lot more lame

nothing approaching i am
                bic or pen tam
        être of course, still
            whatever will be
                what it is to be
                sad to say

catching metrical irregularity
caching an asymmetry in his step
a catachresis of the heart
a thickness of arrhythmia, thrombosis

            at every juncture
            a tick of bones
            a time every
            morning to spell
            crick, crackle,
                        , & pop

where we unravel

five million years a stumble of stars
hydrogen oxygen nitrogen carbon
      a flesh hold on life

             the clack of pilt
down   australopithecus neanderthal
   cromagnon peking in us
     travel and claim
    the disarticulated bones

       your bones, my father,
do not fall into meadows of light
nor waters more supple than skin

the Estevan City cemetery the sound
    clay and gravel make
       the scrape of concrete
         [posture is normally upright
    the bright blood broken

      : : : : :
full fathom five thy father lies
     nebulae & carbon

bone house

inside which we protect
neither ghost nor spirit

    which tear until
    the sun leaks marrow
    tomorrow & to

        morrow time borrows
        the hall warps the mirrors
        before which we move
        and in which wrapped
        as if we were not there

your sorrow, bidden,
quickens, your ankles,
once bitten, click,
like beads, in prayer

castanets in the morning
when you run
into a cascade of yellow
hardy as yarrow
pests cannot kill
nor drought put an end to

you want to live as shadows shed
        as a sparrow
        fishing for light
        as near and as narrow

the body abroad

the body arrives

The body has been tutored
and It has arrIved. It wIll
not leave thIs spot.
If she wasn't here, his friend had said,
someone else would meet hIs body.

Soon a slIm young
body heads toward him.
Yes, the body says.
It looks up, hopefully.
Is It me? Is It I
you are lookIng for?
for whom you are searchIng?

The body wants to be chosen,
lIfts Its eyebrows. Yes?
Up on Its toes. It should transform
Into a bIrd, a crane maybe.
Yes? the body says. Is It I
for whom you are lookIng?
I for whom you send?

It probably Is too eager, the body.
It Is makIng a fool of Itself.

It Is I, here, the body trIes to say. Over
here. Can you hear me? Would you speak to
me? Call and I wIll come,
runnIng.

Someone speeds up. A dog lover? Dog catcher? When he
Is closer the body begIns to shake. The
body can see someone Is holdIng
a sheet of paper. It Is enuff he has come.
Will he know the code?

And then he Is
5 or 6 steps away. Someone holds
up the sheet of paper. The body can make
out the wrItIng. The body pleased,
        makes a few sounds,
he has been found, sought.
The body sees Its name
In a sea of crylIIc.
He knows hIs name.

            DennIs Cooley?
                        yes.
            Pawel Jedrzejko.
The bodIes joIn at the knuckles.
                        HI.
        Thanks for comIng.

body works
(for wolfgang klooß)

          yes, he says, yes, he is in a fit,
            he has to get fit, he might be
          getting fat and what is worse—
         everyone is fat and getting fatter.

       he himself is flatter
       than a spatula, and so to flat
       tery insusceptible, no point fretting
       over his fat & feckless friends.

his life a testimony to stinting, he has renounced all
swilling, scoffed at the smallest joy in bratwurst and nuddlen,
and so prays that never might he beteem the eating of

       he feels great, expects to live
       forever and a day, though
       his trousers no longer fit.

   so fit is he when he walks he flutters
   his bones rattle when he
   flings against his back a knotted rope
   in spiritual struggle and middle-age
   crusades against the body.

   he has taken flight from
   the sullied and disappointing world,
   its soft, warm, and voluptuous tissue
   has confiscated his own imperiled body,
   and in scorn dissolved it.

   he is all scapula, tibia, all
   femur, patella, dos ossos,
   and will at any moment break
   into hornpipe and a cappella.

In hairshirt pride & rectitude,
he renounces old friends,
Falstaffs all of them,

puts his lips to his femur and blows—
his long leg a flügelhorn from the coldest
mountains far above the sordid and too too-solid world—
blows into the high sweet purity of the Alps

,,,,,,,,,,,,,,answering voices
no other can hear, he croons—

sings to a world he holds
in utter contumely.

celestial coordinates

i suppose that is what it is
49.802015600, -97.136199900
a northern story after all
star charts we are mapped on

you send young lawyers & accountants
who are to drag me from sleep
men of eminent sense from London
self-possessed emigres from love
where the red and assiniboine meet
the dried edges of their lives

it belongs to the nineteenth-century,
they grow resolute in etiquette & maps.
you hold candles, roseate, attentively,
prayers in drawing rooms. chapels.
dread noon, the sweating in the ears.

tell me you do not notice
a quickening in their wives
they find fearful and exciting

a tremour on the upper lip
the warm smell of bodies
heavy as milk

annunciation

¥
:Joseph she said and she heard
a wind over all the hills she had ever known
till she was cold and she shivered

and
/quick ,
a fire that was water too

it was like swallowing the sun
over and over and over

¥
she could see
the currents that bent the sky
she would have held
around her against
the nightchill in the sands

she wept and enwrapped herself
found the soft folds in her dress

and out of the wind that touched her
a fragrance and then a very bright light
seeds fell in a swarm of small stars
that were hot & sticky in her hand

the light hit in a shudder that
sounded as if all the camels in all
the Sahara were groaning

¥

i myself do not know if it was so or if
      i saw her late in the day the sun
            swimming in cinnamon
but i know the air was tinged with cloves
and there was the smell of cedars

a simmer in sun and shade until
the streets turned slippery and
astir with sandals and dust
and i remember one corner
         a sundial   \pointing

      ¥

tortoise comb in her hair
she drew in the sands a scorpion
the swollen ache of her longing

she passes braziers smoking with lamb
rosemary and ginger the street stained

pauses at the smell of tangerines
the stall thick with plums in purple skins

the streets taste of burnt molasses
an uneasy & buzzy light
the shame of her desire

¥
the birds from the cliffs
drift like silk in the air and

a prince smooth as the wax from the sun
the sweet odour of camomile
the doves brooding

¥
                    pressed into the stall
        the stink of goat and camel shit
                her dark body
        the nine secret places
            the fluted cry

¥
except it would have been April
dried figs the winds raw and gritty
the streets rutted with wagons

but the body

happy to be body. the body one sunny day gives itself up. stands up from the computer where it was made to sweat & stiffen, next to the window.

whh hh, here body, c'mon body le's go, 'mon boy.

body perks. promises of air & motion. the body stops to get a smell. "'Mon boy, le's go." needn't worry needn't worry. the body follows the leash of his love.

they are buddies now, creatures of der wald, the green and wouldly world, snuffsnuff.

the poet & his body go deeper & deeper, further & further, body talking to itself, talking itself out of its snit. it does not fear ticks, the body. its cold nose sidesteps the little steaming piles that other dogs have dumped in relief and greeting. they wend their way into the warty forest.

the German trees, gummy and roused, are waiting down the shaded paths, rustle rustle, leaning toward them. they want to get the poet alone where they can spray him in the face. he belches poisonous gasses which the trees, grown trembly, inhale in long deep gasps, hhfff hhffhf. they sway in delirium.

but the body. let out, it will not let down the poet. takes him down, yes, to the tennis courts. the body longs to bounce on the balls of its stupid feet. body thinks it is still young, wonders if the poet still loves it. it houghs & makes whimpery sounds, imagines it too could be whacking balls all over the place.

body thinks it could make a run for it. it should fling itself with a rattle against the chain-mail fence where it can cling like a bill-collector or a disappointed soccer fan.

the relique

the man on the radio said
he would give his right arm
to look it in the eye

they could see the time was at hand
and so they played the hand they were dealt
it was a hands-on operation all the way
even for those who dragged their feet

it was no slight of hand there was more
to it than meets the eye
when the tour got off on a solid footing

the student had everything in hand
and hadn't the heart to turn her back on anyone
not even the back-sliders
people were feeling a little down at the heels
but the student was hoping the hand would be
a shot in the arm once they set foot in the room

even so some wondered
would the left hand know
what the right was doing

everyone knew the arm which had left Rome
only a handful of times and had kept an arm's distance
soon would be so close at hand
you could but should not hold
or even touch it, hands off for you

if you got close you could be a relic
in good standing too, fourth class quite probably,
you would be near the steady hand that had shook
the hand of St. Ignatius that had reached out and

touched other hands, warmly,
a life line you could feel in your heart

the student from Ottawa had to watch her step
she kept it at hand in her carry-on and feared
it stood out like a sore thumb where it sat
on the seat the student didn't want the arm
to get off on the wrong foot before she flew it
back on the end of her wrist

organizers did not want to get caught
flat-footed and were glad to find no one
raised a hand certainly not the handful of sceptics
who hadn't a leg to stand on
who for sure didn't want to go to hell
in a hand-basket they would feel like heels
their doubts didn't amount to a slap on the wrist

That is why they stuck their necks out
they pulled it off everyone said
it was a hands-down success

  you've got to hand it to them
  it was a miracle people agreed
  how well things were handled
  it showed the perfect touch

Ulysses returns

enough of this
no more he says
bye-bye sailing to By
zantium this standing by
when creatures go by in 2 x 2
rattling their way to extinction

and who are you to rail
this is no country for cold men
their tired coffee-bean hearts grinding
in an enamel music-box or
inside an oil rig

there should be dolphins of course
& whales cruising plankton
their high mournful songs rising
through the wooden boats
in an aura around the crew
the stars steady and steering

no question of the sharp wind in our wake
salt air & the smell of tar
the wine-dark seas no doubt about that
the somber & tormented waters on which
the waves bosom with ships and mackerel
and stars furl in pennants and release
fires in lapis lazuli

we should expect sirens smack in the middle singing
come live with us come alive with us
the same yeast the same old steamy desire
under a sun that singes and the seas begin
to rise & sweat all over again

there should be more of things
the bazaars jammed with goats & garlic
thick with smoke and buzzings and
voices that shout or whisper
yes and if-only

the rooms where children sing
the small green birds
the warm touch of mothers

Gijon

glass blown full of fish octopus huge squid delicate
speckles a pink sheen a small brown crab and furry big ones flat
gray fish with jagged spines and eyes on top a man, whack, chops
in half, small teeth shiny as wet plastic long fish and faint skin and
ones like tulibees only redder and flatter
a priest, full robes, floats by, shadow under the window
behind the glass some curl like potato peelings baskets
of snails black shells silver sardines rainbow trout the man with
huge scissors quick flick and the guts are gone piles of prawns
huge fish with saggy skin solemn monkfish a skinned fish and the
ones bright as light bulbs would slip in your hands like oil and
tuna after tuna the man heaving their hugeness slices gills, head,
fins, snicks the packed flesh spine after spine with the heel of the
cleaver
three, four, people in an island and the man throwing
ice back over the mounds yes yes the faces nod that one, yes, he
cutting and washing the flash of his movement wrapping the
slippery muscle the ones that are white and flatter than slippers
one large crab breathing upside down in bubbles and clams hairy
with sea weed
men in white look short and out of breath dozens of arms
and dazed on the island of fish singing the women onto the shells
and the bones
in the street the hardbright sun the ocean breeze the light
on the knives the men in white and outside the tall one passing in
black

Le Pétomane

some wait for the gods
everyone waits for Le Pétomane
who did not admit impediments
and did not fritter away his talents

hail to him—blithe spirit—
who looked on tempests and was never shaken
stood behind his loaves of bread
and with an ease that endeared him
to priest and republican alike
leavened them with life

the vapours he had released in them
by the seat of his pants conducted an orchestra
learned to blow out a candle, whoof, happy
birthday, at two paces, let the winds
blow high let the winds blow low
bear him wheresoever they go

to Le Moulin Rouge where having
got his second wind he released
the fine particles in clouds
upon the air he enthusiastically sounded
cannon fire and thunderstorms
and farm animals spoke hiss and grunt
in strange languages through him.
This as he was performing in a silent film.

his was no silent & joyless expression
and so with remarkable ease & gusto
he, patriot, played La Marseillaise
and later could be found, putting on
            airs, to the amusement of
prince and king and country and Sigmund

Freud who by word of mouth had somehow
                    got wind of him
before, dispirited with the slaughter in WWI,
le Pétomane retired to run a biscuit factory in Toulon

the chapel of bones

The man taps his knuckles with his middle finger.
Draws a line of ink. Taps the map.

/Here.

they follow until,

suddenly,

/he falls back.
His voice isn't ready:
"these were.

LIV-ing people!"

They look like a thick-textured rug. Stacked joint-out, so
dehydrated they have sagged in chords of firewood. Bones tossed
onto a window ledge. The face bones seem to have been picked
away, strangely defaced. An intimacy of the living and the dead.

Once smelled salt air, rubbed grit from their faces, tears from
their eyes. Would have felt their legs cramp, heard children crying.
Loved the taste of lemon and lamb, the shiver of desire in the
night. Lost in a repository of minerals.

The blessed, their brittle anonymity held precariously at bay, have
put aside their moments of shining.

may you keep my mother in your arms forever

Theresa loves João

for blessing call Maria 31048

bless me and all my family in our need

Hamlet, Denmark

pray for us in our sorrow

now you gone and done it

may you lift the sickness from my sister's face

call me ~~soon~~ right away

Jose April 1 1911 meet you soon

Brown eyes, so dark they are
almost black, would have visited the world
with a warm light. What is left of them
stares from where, happily, or unhappily,
they once lived.

All over Évora little pools have formed in the stones. They have left
shadows, smooth as water, where their feet had moved.

a sign over the door in Portuguese says:

We Are Waiting For You To Join Us

the young in Coimbra

The days—a string of pearls—
glow with what is new in them.

Taking their own sweet time.
Moving toward one another, they can't
get there fast enough. They have not yet come
down with time.

Will they feel it when it builds
like the soão, starting last night,
a terrible wind in the awning?

    what little is in them,
        the thinness of?

         \time a pail
            \a peril
    \they step into

      a glass they can not see
        themselves in

a disquisition on beauty

Don't talk nonsense, he said. He rubbed his huge fingertips together, with a little more pleasure than was proper, and this is what he said.

Talking talking talking. It must be 2:00 or so, he ridiculing the unbeauty of the poet's body. He talks on, into the night. Drinks and talks, talks and drinks. The poet listens.

The big man with the beard is eloquent when he turns to fine points of female beauty. The poet is pleased. But the man moves on to the most exquisite understanding, the most exacting standards, and the poet grows alarmed.

By now the big guy with the beard is twisting the last drop out of the bottle of Cointreau, which he has drunk entirely by himself. He is sniffing the cork tenderly.

Don't talk nonsense, he says. He sets aside the bottle, the genie out, rubs his fingers together, it's hard to call them tips, they're so large. He touches them with unseemly satisfaction, gazes into the room. He is hardly aware of the poet.

His voice is clear, confident. Don't talk nonsense, poet. What a woman wants in a man is not a svelte and athletic body, he says, and he holds the fingers together, again, exquisitely. It's not that. Women don't want a pretty boy, they're not interested in male elegance. It's not fitness, it's not the same old mesomorph. Forget the smile and swagger. Forget the Vitruvian man. What women want in a man, he says, and he lingers longer than seems right over his fingers, and a long drag on his cigarette—I'll tell you what interests women. What women want most in a man . . . is the capacity to . . . tell a story, a man who can speak with felicity. They want someone who can talk with ease and charm.

It is 3:40 in the morning. He is rubbing the tips of his fingers together.

the inner ear

bring it close—
hold it closer—

like the heron cock
your ear & listen—

the coch lea a snail
-shell, three parts fluid,
two that transmit pressure,
another that like a conch sends
murmurs to the brain.

lucky, you will say—
luck luck luck the water

birds at night, in Oviedo,
a video we replay bright as vireos
in our heads.

Ido ido ido they say
sshhush sshusshh

the cochlea among the ado
and the surging rocks—
swinging with the tides.

the body politic

salt

you know how it is :
how things go :
with sodium

               which and when
once introduced to chlorine
will turn to lung-eating poison
lethal in love or din
airily to young men
shrouded in mud & barbwire.

                  salt that stings
              and salt that cures
              will also purify
                        those who have fallen in.
it is salt that lubricates cells
so that they may move beside & over
amorous with sliding,
sticky with sweat,
a good solution, then,
and may charge batteries.

Salt that seethes the ocean
that preserves the seas in us
the old tides urging

to tears that sting & crust
preserve our love of sorrows
from rusting & slings of

salt that keep
the horses standing—
standing armies fed—

in lack of which walls
flimsy as slats collapse

salt that keeps us
dumb & patient
slow cattle licking
at our thoughts

salt that will lend savour
flavour to the kitchen,
or if we but sprinkle it
over the shoulder or
under the sheets
will bring luck
and a little pleasure.

     salt they drew from
    water 8,000 years ago prevents
    infection from spreading, prevents coming
        down with disease—
    a silting in with death.

we, being the salt of the earth,
felicitous in what we do
and what we say, seasoned,
spend our days licking
our wounds

the unbearable
dehiscence we dare—

        looking back—
      to call love.

across the line

what is it to be
living in america's attic—
a bright cloud of snow,
a windy blindness,
stray dogs sniffing
„these are the particulars of north.

small creatures who at night scratch
initials & scribble graffiti
on the inside of your skull—
a tick stuck in the brain.

what it is to live where cold clicks
at the pane and sticks
in your eye like a pick.

what it was to go
"across the line"
over the 49th parallel
on what we called "a 48."
what it meant to know
the boundary was "The Medicine Line"
that protected the Dakota Sioux,
and that far to the north, in summer solstice
the light never quite disappears
unread by those on the ground floor
who do not notice the ceiling on their days,
or the faint scuttling on top of their dreams—
    who do not feel a shiver from the draft

when talking to ourselves.
we come down the stairs—
we are watching our steps,
knowing you will not know
          who we are, but you will know
          that we have crossed the line—

          that we were there,
              we are here,
                  that's us—

                      pissing yellow
                  letters in the snow.

immunity

the system knows
who you are not, it remembers
you well, and it will
defend against all those
who are not you,
who resent you for what
they think you so recently are.

there can be no impunity
before their mutinous ways, no preventing
the ridges they lay across your nails,
nor hair floating to the floor in small drifts.
beware beware his flashing eyes, his falling hair,
his knobby knees, his shoulders seized.

believe—if you can—
the body's mute recalcitrance
to invasion and take-over,
to munitions & ordnance.

the body—puny when it comes to old friends
in alias who ((alas those, inter alia,
once repelled infiltrators that tried
to seize its neck & elbows,

who now confused grow
uncertain about who is who
and what is where

especially you, who look more
and more like someone who might
not be you and someone not to be
trusted, who has upped his defences,
or a lot like me, suspected someone
of not being who they thought.
or (once) pretended.

Julio Portillo's body

the pope in purple so grand
his robe could be from tincture stained
the grapes glowing with prophecy

the people must leave politics must not
concern themselves with murder & mutilation
when it bursts in their mouths the sour wine
will ease the lesions that scour Julio
Portillo's body says the pope
in remembrance of

says your hands my people
full of bruises are plums your heads
under the bulb on the prison's cord are
circled in halos sanctified for you
are legion for you are as is Christ
sacred your scars your sacrament
when they flood the land with
estuaries of your blood
and all things red become
diluted in Mary's blue

the pope promises all things will be
brought to light so also
Julio Portillo's body
will also see the light

the purple man says blessed be
the pilgrims who forage for ages for God
will appear in their hands as a lamp
a candle fragrant with incense
a forgiving hand and for dreams of sin
it will burn out your eyes

(*Julio Portillo, Salvadoran math teacher and union activist)

newsreel

it takes about that long

someone puts some
thing on the man's chest
someone wants there

someone watches &
they point things at him
they stick things in him
the figure jerks
surprised it is still there

sleepy almost, it is falling,
asleep it   slowly droops
its bones   turn to water

all this slowly on film

        it is not you it is
          some else it is
      some thing in you

            you are on
        the news tonight

        you are a small
            wet splat

pope orders priests to quit politics

(1)

sinister is a

sun a can

ister of gas

their sister twelve on Friday

hit by the bomb

it could be napalm

a blister in the palm of her hand

psalms, a holy lamp lit

a wicked burning   with thanks

that palm plantations will remain
in the hands of Del Monte & generals
they will not be stigmatized

it is their will

there will be

alms or no alms

she will be a plant
a yarrow of light
she will be a glass
filled with water
more clear than light

or gas

she will be compliant

past complaint

she will she be

a fragrant fire   will sing

in her limbs

the word will sing

& singe

holes in her body
in her blood she will be
washed & hung
in the tenement
she will be
a shining example to all others

(2)
she is not a pomegranate
though she is the colour of a plum
she is not a garnet   or a poppy

for her there is no
haven she finds no heaven
she is not whole
nor is she holy

she does not burn
with a gem-like flame

when she is spun in their spit
her soul does not burst on fire
her body when she burns
stinks
like pork
imparts no balm

penny wise

the man they hung according to
the paper the peters & the paupers
folded like an accordion when he
held up the bank in Plum
Coulee and the manager closed
around the hole in his belief

it was spring he was sprung
the earth flung loose from penury
the banks in god's purpose overflowing
with savings accounts the world
aspill with April and an apricot sun

it was a terrible blow to safe
keeping the trust in legal tender
he had smashed his leg
(accidentally) when he fell
escaping the doctor
who (incidentally) worried when
he said he would
never walk again

when all he had intended
was for Penny meant
to be sitting pretty
to send good news
the leg so well & tenderly mended
the doctor thought to have
saved him when
he would be up to the walk
all the way on his own

all the way to the o-zone
to the letters he would poke his head into
and they would throw the lasso around him
(accidentally on purpose) in the end
once they got the hang of it
a priority to draw him (blithely)
four sheets to the wind
time was up they said and
(deliberately) hung him

      like Billy Budd
      like a union jack

BJ: a tie game

~

four sheets to the wind
                    that's him
never listened
                            never learned
never cared
                        to mind his tongue
            never tried
        caveat or no caveat
tired of cravats and grammar

you couldn't tell him a thing
he was bound to take a header

                    ~
            refused to be con
            trite /right &
            look where it got him

    \that's where he made a big mistake
            right then & there they had him
                    where they wanted

                ~
if only to correct his speech his bad
spelling his affront to taste they would
loop ink on a paper
choose the letters that would
tell him where he belonged

they dressed him up in a suit
gray as weathered ship
he should have been proud
he should have leapt /rejoicing

~

you would have thought he'd have come to his senses
                                                but no
              he was dressed to the nines
        he was dressed to kill

~

  at the big dance he was decked
      in a fancy necktie   the dandy

he had really tied one on
he swore to god this
would be his last hang over

~

        he became a
                        bit heavy-footed
                    when he slipped
              through a crevasse in the air

he was quite a hunk you have to admit
                    & his breath
it will astonish you to hear his breath

        /snapt

body works

the winter of their discontent

souls entered the world as lost
flames and stinking of cinders,
names pinned to their backs
wide-eyed & fluttering.

in the first cold snap
they shrank and suffered frost bite—

their noses ran & their mittens
            hung on strings,
their scarves matted with their breath
they sniffled and wiped
their noses on their sleeves.

when the neighbours who could read
the addresses sent them home,
            solid as snow balls
the sun had become an aspirin
and they were puffing bright clouds.

            a few souls would drop in—
            once in awhile you would see them
            visiting over coffee at the kitchen table.

                  quite a few were tickled
                  pink to be cabbage,
                  for a moment, to be
                  bulgy and wet with flesh.

Fort-Da

here it is, now—
       here it is,
            ,, not there
  / here.

can't you hear it
right here and now—
now is the time—
is it not there then.

it's now or never,
you say, & who is to say
how it will play out—
how the lines are cast
or will ever meet.

  here it is, now,
       you know it is—
time to reply knowing it is
    neither here,   nor there,

      here we are—
nowhere else and you know it.

      it is there, now—
        there there
  i say.
              and so it goes—
      so it is

        there it is

  there you go, then.

lost at sea

the brain, being conscious, must know
what it is to levitate in a basin of bone
to paddle in mineral puddles
for warmth and for coolness
to dip within grief and desire

it realizes the world's contagions
will, unbidden, boil over,

it is a blue bottle
a Portuguese man o' war
drags its venom across
the salt-stained body
sheltering small creatures,
        killing most

            it is an octopus,
          courteous, curious,
      lured unsuspecting into a pot
    from which, desculpa, it will be
      scooped to sudden death

it is an old man with white legs
he dangles into the river
his feet are dirty & boney
they stir small circles in the mud

woman in love

the partridges jolt
from their sleep

the fox wraps
the blood it has stolen
round her neck

the fox,
under her
coat, eats a hole
out of her side—
she'd rather
die than say

the rank odour of pain
lopes the fields
slopes the ravines

bright eyes   bright teeth
adrenalin breath

let there be light

*

let there be light she/he said
without let-up—
huge arms full of it,
bright as brand-new glass from Glasgow,
more than you might guess or imagine.

the world lissome, the yeast brewing—
the sweet arcing fire.

*

you probably have heard stars,
when they age increase in luminosity,
and they pour out champagne
faster than a ship lost in the north atlantic—
& that this bodes
ill for all bodies
swarming over the hull.

*

in the meantime, the boulevard
of cracked tiles hums and sparkles
in Barcelona, and the sunlight
splashes through the windows
in the Sagrada Familia.

*

and here people flicker and whoosh
like dandelions in the broken streets,
brighter than tropical
fish—brighter than gaudi—
among the coral.

*

you would be amazed
how steadily they burn—

and how one day they will turn
blue in the night.

the angels arrive

                    would be tempted
                 to say the tremendous
                 and pendulous earth

hangs on a plum line dropped
from god's palm wound up
& down by a squabble of angels

who land in a haze of sweat & nectar & mosquitoes
in saskatoons that ping into honey pails
spiders that turn black and burn in our ears

the poem would say those
things and saints would billow
a sufficient number would crash
find themselves splattered on the street
they were sent to baptize
directly in front of sutherlands plumbing

all of them, the poem would realize,
have to sizzle in the crabapple dark
they would be baffled and lose direction,
those sent in compensation or in consolation,
who have been capsized from the ark

the poem couldn't help noticing
the clouds milling and smelling of angel's feet
could hear them shake the rain from the clouds
the yard crammed full of thready stuff

the poem would feel compromised
there would have to be
spirits with ruby throats
who at night shudder
ruddy as merganser ducks
scudding in for a landing

the latest edition

something odd and add
ended or tacked on

it's hide & seek
it's hard to say

the errors in your seam
stress what ever is left
when the body is uncrated
the appendix redacted
the stitches popped

who then the sun
who the squatting moon
its splatter of piss
who knows
the equator's noon
the cratered tune

who cares much of anything
about the unseemly world
the desecrated, uncreated body

ex libris

the brain hoards its keepsakes
like tickets to the opera

> the body runs
> a messy library
> under the dim bulb
> the pages ripped & dog
> eared, some gone missing,
> whole books stained with thumb
> prints, coffee spills, squashed flies
> the dribblings of cheese & dandruff,
> words eaten by mice and dimmed by mold,
> whole rooms eventually lost to flood and fire.

some holdings burnished
lovingly with blue & gold
in cowled and monkish devotion
some sections so badly scribbled
and written over no one can tell
what might once have been printed there.

beribboned

First there was something, and then
that something became something else.

i.
the cell from which we remake ourselves
is in the video turning out
pipe cleaners and sponges
fuzzy insects, giant, it is
returning us to ourselves
turning us out too.

    the loops & coils peel
    like metal from a lathe—

the machine zips, unzips
its ceremonies of spin & copy
          busy little jig
    transcribing versions
         & revisions of us

ii.
the fly catchers hung in strips
dropped from the ceiling
in curls big as Shirley Temple's,
cartridges from which they unwound
in gummy membranes, turned
black with the dead bodies
that had burned in small, hot engines.

iii.
    candy in long ribbons,
     curled on itself—red
   & white cinnamon burned
    his tongue at the Odd
    +Fellows' Christmas

iv.
the smooth, shining ribbons—
a kid of 12 and on his jacket
pinned red & blue & white
his sister claims still
to have in a box a picture of

v.

   in hospital, hallucinating

cloth and thread. reams and reams, the women in confidence and
bearing. gossamer piling up. filament filament filament. silk in the
breeze

two women move easily as streamers from one tall building to the
other, the two women, without walking or riding. combing the
fine fabric, long skeins on the air, whiff of spices.

for heaven's sake, her husband says.

the two women winnowing, winnowing.

v.

   the black ribbon
   that appeared
   on his body

listen

you and i both know it is
time to get the lead
            out completely
necessary to act with aplomb,
to be blithe with bleifrei
                        also fealty

            also: nothing
wrong with your secret & sludged-up heart
the result of a faulty and ill-kept carburetor
nothing that an oil change or a new spark

            plug a good tune
up wouldn't hurt no need to
inhale so deeply nor to swoon
the fumes of your own exhaustion

i'd be pleased to hear you idling
behind the door before it swings
            open with a rattle &
                        // there you are

            a new ease
a marvel of transmission

            the satisfying
glissade of sleeve and piston

the idea of order at due north

arms and legs thinning
  hair too until he
begins to look
  like a tin
can, a water
    tower, a sand
        hill crane

among the twists of weeds and glass,
a stiff wind through scabby trees.

the ends of his lines
     jerk so badly,
his life has beome a stiff wind
he drags behind.

     he is a yo
-yo, unable to return,
  and so pirouettes,
       as if in court.

has known from the very first—
    he has been running
      out of time.

body parts

*

yeahyeahyeah   back there
look i ain gonna wait on yuh hand & foot
way back there somewheres.

you mean you dont know
it was apparent he didnt & so
we rummaged our way through
a graveyard of salvaged parts
he'd saved almost everything.

*

we had to be careful not to step
on the eyes—there were bags
& bags of eyes right by the counter—
Beheaded people staring at us,
& some of them had got squished.

we found a cart
Mike & Gabe & Zeke & me,
& we got started.

wasnt easy without help &
we hadnt done anything
like this before, but we started chucking.

*

toes patellas posterior vena cava ankles arteries,
they had a lot of nerve, stacks & stacks of it,
like spaghetti & a partsman with a fistful of it
also brains, bins & bins of brains
sitting on the shelf stupid as walnuts or
magnetos with their wires crossed or gone
hay wire & all kinds of bones in boxes

all kinds of teeth a big collection of teeth (yellow)
that rattled like cotter pins or dominoes
a lot of kidneys skulls shaved
& shelved dusty headlights in small
town garages, cases of cheeks & chins it was all there
gall bladders stacked by the millions,
a big stock of bladders vertebrae like garlic or
nuts on wire hoops down one aisle trays full of girdles
lines & lines of spines strung up
                    to cure at the end
intestines drooping like water slides
livers idle as abandoned chemical plants,

hormones were spectacular, cortisone too—
insulin throxine adrenaline testosterone
estriol estradiol estrogene progesterone—
the place bright and ankle-deep with them.

                    *

            I'm telling you,
            it was all there—
            the miraculous display
            cases of greens
            & blues in crystal rows

            we got a lot of that,
            that & jaws—there was
            a special on jaws
            so we got some extra—
            but it was awful
            hard to get fresh muscle.

we blushed when we hit the
Venal Section   & rushed
right past—fast as we could—
so we got those pieces pretty
mixed up, I am afraid,
when we pushed them in alongside
the long slide of pelvic girdles.

                        how much blood?
dunno—20, 30, litres or so, I guess—
& we got that too. Gabe dipped
a great big ladle, yea long,
out of a cask into an empty pail

                    *

we picked up a lot of things at Cosmic Wreckers,
where we stood in the pools under the stomachs.

In one room a bunch of guys
on a doo-hickie like they fix shoes with
were polishing knee caps
& tossing them into compartments—
shiny as hub caps.

Some others lazing 'round in the back room got
knuckles all over the table—
one guy digs in his pocket & out comes
                    a fistful of knuckles.

we pick up just about every damn thing,
but nowhere any skin glue—no
warranty, no customer service, no
guarantees on parts or service—
there weren't even any air pumps

for the lungs we found stashed
like hot water bottles under the cages.

*

the guy in charge couldn't care less—
he had a monopoly, he didn't have to.

so we check through the register—
gonna haf ta get yr own water buddy
& he, Pete, his name 's Pete, he's workin'
for The Man, crams all the stuff
into a big bag of skin

as we leave, the gates close
behind us, & we see something glimmering
with anger in the air waving
behind us, & I get this sickening
feeling we arent going to pull this off—
somethings left out we've left
something behind back there
where the broken bodies are stripped
down & hearts leak
all over the floor.

*

we done our best since,
but you got
to forgive me—

i cant help wondering
about all those hearts.

as the spirit moves us

*

you dear reader don't know
a thing about gas
ping for air and the pass
ing of wind a passing fancy
you may suppose

the stiff wind from the west
a rumour of the far shore
the priests fondling entrails
the cats pissy with excitement

they do not give a flying fart for poetry
said the notes at best would be flat
would not ring on the stars
nor bring on the rain

it is confluence that is wanted
the pneuma touching down as a gift
the soul a cool blue flame
eyes luminous as tropical fish

*

this be no inadmissible art nor cause
to look down one's nose at, or hold,
even if false would be surely permissible
one big round one, firm as the devil's,
confident as a turnip and as profound,
one good thumper that hits
the floor with a satisfying thud

it was best, the best flatologists deduced
a jostling, a jousting for air
as in ribbons snapping
on timbrel & drum
in jest & manner a Hera
clitean fire

      *

the poet must watch his step, keep his feet,
if ever he is to dance the eight-toed romance
when lightning strikes the dark and thunderous heavens
the rumblings deep inside the earth

to bring a breath of fresh air
in the night produce a noble gas
paint the world a bright helium
in argon and xenon

      *

would they like one sturdy as a stool
or a long plaintive one
so pained it would madden your soul
a keening to cow a piper

some wait for staccato or
trilling piccolo in fingering
the thin sigh of life, an oboe,
a tight-throated tug boat also

it's a long time looking,
they agree, it's
a long way home

for that matter

                                what of:

                      —Chlo

               Rine:

toxic as an adder
its sting

                —So:

)in due proportion,
a few grains per diem(

                  Dium:

So Dium and Chloe Rhine
in a delirium, perturbed,
on their own dime

              which when thrown
              into water will blow
                 you to bits you
                  should not be

            surprised to get caught
            in this position to know
                that on their own
                 left to their own

devices they incite
the very end of things

                  —still, these two
           invite (the amatory pro)
            (clivities the won)
         (derful civilities of things)

once domesticated will wait
       meekly upon table
amen able and ready
will flavour meals
in a saving grace
and with their plea
sure favour though we
       spend savour salt

anatomy of melancholy

sadness moves into the shoulders.
it stays up maddeningly
late and will not pay the rent.
sadness refuses to clean up
the joint, forms a coalition
with lumbago & claims tenant rights.

sadness has friends in
long after visiting hours,
and installs them in high places,
with smelly feet and tobacco breath
they settle in determined as carpenter ants.

sadness holds the body hostage
sucks the milk of human kind
ness sulks in the marrow of the bones,
eats too much, too messily,
and puts on weight.

when sadness is feeling really low
it begins wearily to climb
the ladder of your ribs.

at night Cooley listens

at night he listens to his body
an answering service he bends over
the rest of the time he does not listen, his neglect shameful

the body becomes importunate spouse
it's about time you listened to me
the body rehearses a long list of grievances, sniffling
                        & there are violins

      he hopes the body will not leave him,
      however unfaithful he would be

      sometimes his body tries to reason with him
                              its sockfoot honesty
      listen im not gonna take this any longer
      I could go to the police you know

         one terror after another
      the body engages in hit & run tactics

      when do i get the smallest bit of love
      you never spent a nickle on me
      you cheap bastard

      there was a time the poet was proud
      to be seen with his body
      dressed it in a tan & open shirts

      he looks into the body's eyes
      knows there must be truth there
      naked as a newly polished car, hurtful,
            a flute quickens faintly off stage

real bad i got it bad this time
the little prick malingers & feints
sabotages every night out
stores up evidence for all-night recrimination
the body comes home bitching & ungrateful

     thump thump—the poet's heart is a kettle
     then faster & louder a snare drum
     he is tossed on the adrenalin
     it washes ashore, sweeps at his feet
     his fear squirts like a carburetor
     he hears oboe hears panic he is a man
     whose kid has run into the street, not looking

     hurt hurt hurt the body cries and turns saxophone
     it can't hold on much longer says 12 strings says
     I'm goin' down Mister & I'm
     takin' yuh with me you & yr abuse

       the poet angles for time
     he has poems to write fantasies to fant

     body renews its grievances
     i'm yr body ain't i
     we go back a long time you & me
     why you doin' this to me

                he knows death
            has fallen overboard and it cries
        out in the hot chambers of his heart

they wrangle for hours
until they tire at last are tender
in the long late night they are close
Cooley & kidney inmates of death
Cooley tearful the body might leave him

        the two of them making sorrow
            full music talking
                  it over,

             intimately,
all night long

their startling beauty

look for the rusted nails
check for the knubby digits
you can hear the birds brooding,

listen for the snapping
ribs, the chattering
heart you can know only as a lark
in a dark tree a few vertebrae
singing Tenebrae when you
yank open the hatch and lug them
home as keepsakes, roll them
in the palm of your hand,

you should be grateful when
the room splinters and you rouse him
from his fever, relieve him of the yellow nails,

you should know that
when your ears are cold as midnight beetles
they will form a wen in your side, a gall,
a burl which when rubbed releases
a startling beauty you can add to your relics,

you should walk him until he does not need you and you
yourself come down with a lethargy more viscous than tar,

perhaps when he sits up
          the nails will
          fall from his wrists,

                              eat this,
                         it's my last
                         he will say—
                    he was meant to say.

to be in

in, but not of, the brute
and surd world turning
every fall among
the dry corn and the earth
throwing up summer
squash with pale dirty bums

you should but do not
shudder when the day
thuds into you

when in a loud crack it snaps
in tin-snip and turn-buckle
and rain splatters the yard

when the wind shatters
and the hail skitters like dice

that's when you puddle
in half-hearted steps
and your scalloped-potato
heart slumps inside the porch

supplicant

pray for protection from the night.

you who made a run for it
and greatly rejoice
in renunciation the ruin of
what once you
held like a joy.

nun on a bed of nails—
you have slain the commotions
that have shaken you.

all night long you wake and finger
the bright beads of blood.

the machinery of his breathing
(for Steven Ross Smith)

a burble of air and the ear comes ungummed.
the body consents to coughs & splutters.

the body wheezes and scrapes day
and night moans and sometimes it hisses.
when it closes its eyes it rises
on tip-toe and keens like a hungry gull.

the body devotes its life
to sniff & snore, trusts to spit & spatter.
the body knows what it stands for.
it believes in squeaks and clacks .

the body persists until it
shudders and begins to stutter—
threatens to expire in glug & snort.

when the body spots an artic owl
it sings to itself in a low, happy hum.

they find their tongues

the throat finds new shapes,
at first clumsy and slow, and after—
   : light , more fluent

they stick their tongues out—
learn to spell in clicks & buzzes—
the parabolas of frogs, the parable of crickets.

the flesh bulges and folds—
floods them with blood.

he listens, drinks the warm words
   , their milky effluence
stupefied with message.

when her chest winnows
past her ear, he puts
his lips to her lips

they are involved in one another,
the small canal traces,
the nerves and nevers,
the windy ridge their collar bones make.

quite the whopper

right elbow in left palm
forearm straight up

shakes the forearm
back & forth as if
it were a cudgel

that guy he had a
wang on him
                    /that long

& a girl can't
be too careful

now a days
you can't be
she sez you
can't be
too careful
you know

or ever get
too lucky

first thing you know

i.
first thing you know, folks get wind of it—
the feisty lady, one part fist, one part fart,
Old English "fyst" (to fart) and
German "fist" (a small excitable dog)

ii.
Who? Arnason asked.
Asked W.O. Mitchell.
Mitchell eager to write a new novel
to match the wonts of junior high.
What are you going to call it Bill:
"Who Has Passed the Wind"?

iii.
also (as scholars know and can attest) a disheartening act:
petard: a small bomb used to blast down a gate or a wall, which
can of course backfire, a loud fircracker, from French péter (to
break wind), from Latin peditum (a breaking wind), from pedere
(to break wind). Ultimately from the Indo-european root pezd-
(to break wind) which also gave us feisty, fart, and the French
pet (fart). Hence the peterman? Peter Peter, legume eater. And Le
Pétomane?

iv.
not to mention (as is common knowledge):
    a) a wind break on the prairies, an attempt to stall god's
       illimitable temper
    b) as much chance as a fart in a bag of nails
    c) a collection of: some bottled, some canned, some preserved,
       for now if not eternity. an acclaimed collection, cherished
       by fundamentalists, consisting of whispers shouts
       sounds of air exhaled through hairy noses and whiskers,
       the expulsion of evil spirits & freed spirits returning
       enthusiastically to the lord

v.
in addition (as physics attests):
    1. gas can have no fixed shape or volume
    2. yet is it subject to Important Gas Laws
    3. known as The Ideal Gas Law and others
    4. The Laws of Boyle & Charles & Gay-Lussac & Dalton too
    5. Watch Now: Physical and Chemical Properties of Matter

the best that is said

let us agree the animal
gathers its darkness & goes
its way crazed
by fleas & itches

it loves to hear
and to bear us away
gloves & all takes
our very and every breath
untwists & throws it
across the pommel
in a blanket to warm us

set in its ways
off into the sun
the sweet no
-sweat by & by

oh give us this
day our daily breadth
give us a whole bunch
a big spread of bread & cheese
a sip of cognac or anise

arise then and find
a little rice, a nice bed
the best that is
the best that is said

more breath than we got
more than we ever knew
& we will not bite the dust
once we know

death in the home stretch
is breathing hard & farting

back gammon

It's all coming back to me.
Back when life was good.
Get back that loving feeling.

We go a long way back.
As far back as you can remember.
Looking back I might have done things differently.
But now we're back.
We're right back where we started.

You can't hold back the rain.
You can't hold back the sunrise.
You can't hold back the wind.
You are back where you belong.
Blinking back the tears.

You have bounced back.
Back in the game.
Sit back and enjoy it.
Back in my arms.
Sit back and relax.
You are back.
Back home again.
Back home where you belong.

        I always knew you'd come back.
        You always come back.

the fact of the matter

What's the matter with you?
-Nothing, not a thing. It doesn't matter.
Of course it does, it's a matter of life and death.
-What does that matter? Why should i care?
Listen, it's no laughing matter.
-As if it really matters.
It's a matter of record.
-When you get down to the matter, it doesn't, it doesn't matter one little bit. It's immaterial to me.
You have no idea what really matters, do you?
-It's a matter of conscience. A matter of opinion, and I have my own views on the matter.
Yes, and you refuse no matter what.
-I have given the matter some thought. Do i have any say in the matter?
Everyone does. It is a matter of principle, a matter of looking things up, being informed. What's the matter with that?
-Well, no matter what, it makes no sense.
Let's stick to the matter at hand, which is close and candid. The reason why doesn't matter much.
-No. No matter the price. No matter what happens. No matter what it takes. You have confused the matter.
Well, that's a whole other matter, isn't it?
- As a matter of fact it was simply given to us—a handful of dust and no explanation, not really.
Maybe we could settle the matter. Let's close the door on the matter.
-Nah. No matter how slim, there is always a chance. No matter how you look at it.

Let's stick with the matter, shall we?
It's only a matter of time.
No matter what.

summer dream

The body, a cistern, and beside it, a pump.
We understand that. It is easy to see.
The pump is on all the time, night and day.
The belt slaps against loneliness.

It is the pump in the movie,
an urgent muffled sob.
You can hear it at night—
throb throb throb
And the woman, restless, she too—
She can hear it. So can you, dear reader.

          The pump chugging, a fever.
       The far yard between.
She rubs against the darkness.

She has sat alone in the warm night, looking out.
The insects ticking against the screen,
gluing themselves to the light.

She has risen and left
       the porch when the truck pulled up
       throaty motor and she has walked
       down the steps down the sidewalk to
       the street where the trees hunch inside
       themselves. She has leaned into the
       darkness in the window the music
       from the radio low and warm she has
       leaned for the longest time where the
       truck shudders into the darkness

She returns, blouse open,
　　　breasts bare,

　　　　in the thick night
　　　　she is drowning in fire.

the heart of the matter

spiffy

her heart a flask,
a mickey dazzler
she pulls from her pocket,
want a snort?
a nifty glass in which she presents
the essence d'amour.

get a jiffy on, she says,
here, have a sniff,
if you know what's good.
                & when she
                   squeezes,
              the left vent
            ricle wheezes—

                      whiff whiff it sez
              her breath a moist whisper,
        a bright sigh that says
            coriander   sandalwood   tobacco

         , have a sniff.

you and your dried-pea heart

who am i to deride
the hard little seed you chew,
when you screw up your face and spit
down the straw of your welcome.

what's needed is
a good soaking, a little
liquefaction of the heart

that will glisten
brighter than a leopard frog,

swell with desire,
in one gulp swallow
my bluefly affections.

overtaken

i know in overtures
you like to think
you are a sink
full of water
& i an over
turned bottle

infested with dead crickets
and soggy cigarette stubs that
you can save and return for the deposit,

the glass as you can see is marred
until no one can tell
where it's from or what's inside,
the gray and watery letters
beyond the scour of your wire-brush attentions,
behind the mirror you think to find yourself in
a manuscript praising your genius & your beauty.

i would have bobbed straight to you
in the swishy wake of your disaffection
a small ship about to crack and go under,
could also be a boulder beneath which worms breathe,
and small beetles sing blackly
and the dents in the earth close
sadly to your thoughts.

everything a soft dough you take
under your cookie-cutter care,

you will find me suffering
seismic tremours, shaking
from the rumours you spread,
the slab of dissuasions you have
back-packed like Hannibal
over the mountains,
and down like Moses

until in a sickening *plock* you
plunk me with a stone,
and down i go in a gulp,
a windjammer lost on the waves,
a tramp steamship spewing smoke,
and a slew of bad memories.

your heart exposed

will lose its moxy,
its epoxy soon enough.
will swear off its roseate glow,
shrivel into a dead toad on a gravel road.

you will pinch out at least one
pink pearl of caring
before it ends in air so foul
it would choke the oil sands,
besmirch the stars with charcoal.

when the cat chews ardently
at your gristled heart
you will grow weary of being
a metaphor, which is one more
iteration of the same
old story, and you will be back
thwacking against the lid.

that is the moment you will cry out—
this the moment you will always remember.

mayhems of the heart

millions of them fail every year,
hawing and hemming.
her own heart once solid as garlic sausage
and jammed into a smoker was well
on its way to fears he might,
like a magpie, sing and in aria
lay siege to her ear.

we must surface as a seal
at the breathing hole, he said,
we must learn to practise
the many mayhems of the heart,
when the animals appear
and dance in the sun.

she should consider the holes in his heart,
which if she were but to touch
would sound light as a flute,
warm or glow like a lamp
which her scorn sizzles,
instead, like a bratwurst until
like a bagpipe it bursts out wailing.
and her failing once-fat heart goes brick-red

you are pretty good, she said,
awfully good, aren't you,
when it comes to collusion
when it comes right down to it,
when it comes to crushing
all the cartilage in a girl's heart.

to give a little

                         tug on the frayed cord
                        dangling from behind
                 and under your seized-up heart.
                  small bulb that should squirt
                in your armpit like a turkey baster

you would say i was trying
to pull a fast one, and wonder
when i yelled, would the birds shoot
up with a clacking sound
according to the third
law of thermodynamics—
would i crack a smile
and ignite your heart,

or you, yourself, when i give
another yank or two to
that little two)or four
-stroke engine you have
been keeping in the toolshed
coated with dust & grease.

        would you give
          your self a little
            shake, would you
                cough—blushingly—until
                in a spume of exhaust
                you shuddered to life.

help for the lovelorn

you heartless bastard, she said,
have you no feelings for me—
I have heard you rumble like a rutabaga—
your heart in winter clack like a walnut,

> it's a lack, I'm saying,
> a spiritual malaise—
> and I'm sick of it.

he realized something was needed—
a change of heart called for—

knew one day when it came down
to it he would plunk himself
smackdab on a slab when his heart
was no longer in it, and they would
pick it up like a sweet potato, his heart,

or a bowling ball from the gutter,
as in sacrifice or propitiation
a cherished relic in a glass sacellum,
and brought out on birthdays
and twice on Groundhog Day.

also a blood-red gem, prized as
the Black Prince's Ruby—
which is not a ruby but a large
irregular cabochon red spinel
seized by murder from Granada—

also a scuffed rugby ball
hauled all the way to Canada—
his heart a small ham
packed on ice and
set aside
for the staff picnic.

[please insert   or remove
whatever figure you choose
dear reader   ?what harm in that]

ms. lonelyhearts

has the heart you treat as
a motor sprung a leak
is it dripping oil better
fix it today before it is too late
do not ignore it or hope
it repairs itself be proactive

left unchecked it can get on hoses or seals
and cause them to degrade prematurely
leaking oil can create ugly smudges
your engine could suddenly
seize up or burst into flame

you should not feel disheartened
it is crucial to stop the leaks
that should be your number one priority

for starters have a peek under the hood
you should keep a close eye on the dipstick if
the level drops you are losing

oil when blue smoke pours out
check for signs of stains or a puddle
especially after it has been sitting

overnight crawl under and check the oil
pan you are looking for gaskets that have failed
be sure that the plug is tight
and the bolts on the pan are snug

a little care for your own condition
and by morning you will be
back in circulation
and singing like a top

his heart, awry

i.

> what's wrong   with you, she said
>   on Remembrance Day
> when he said it was noisy,   his heart,
> it had run away on him—

when it huddled like a hungry pig
it choked up water in rusty spasms
and it sounded like an old pump
it sounded as if it were   the motor
in *Ryan's Daughter*   low and throbby
   tthh-rru ump   tthhrump
and the lovers at night ran   out to meet

it was also, he thought, but did not say,
a truck with failed brakes.

noisy nothing, she said,
he had it   coming, and
    so she   sent him.

ii.
his feelings sloshed in a swampy heart,
and someone said please,

    lie down

       /here—

      there—
   on your side.

and she touched him   gently
husshha hhuusshuh it said, his heart,
though it would not shush—
it slushed in unseemly ways,
could have been a rowboat,
and he splashing clumsily with oars
when she rubbed   his chest
                                            here

              and   there,

    softly, and sometimes
                  slid her   hand over—
          brushed   his neck,
          slid her hand over
his stomach—his heart
wheezed like an asthmatic
breathed like a bellows—

he heard whumps and gurglings,
sounds of the distant shore filled with gravel,
he thought of Matthew Arnold listening
with a heavy beard to the long dreary roar, and
his heart flapped like a raincoat
in a prairie west wind.

sometimes he recognized the squeaks
were a balloon that rubbed among the shrubbery,
something else that jostled and shuttled
one that fretted like the prickly porpentine.

he heard feet   in rubber boots
sucking mud   where they ran
              a sump pump,
one time he heard   thin little farts.

iii.

it was his   heart he heard
under her   hand, his heart
shivered with nearness—
a grenade before they pulled the pin.

she played   the valves
to his great-big tuba heart,
ran her fingers round the rim
the music was   coming from
the neck in a   bottle,
in a sigh   or hiccough
sometimes the clear
notes of an archangel.

the keyboard   clicked—
his hurt   heart gushed
sanguine as   the salty seas,
nimble as a porpoise, it splashed—
        or a baby orca,
      playful, curious
      the promise of—

iv.

wait here,   she said,
        standing up.
we will send   the results
                        /to your doctor.

he returns

she was not surprised when he said
each breath at night caught him
off guard, he heard

the air when his chest moved,
a ship rose in bubbles that
squeaked against each other,
wet cracklings that could be candy,
peanut brittle softly breaking.

he heard wheezy sounds in the throat,
small gasps in the sternum,
the complaint of block and tackle
noticed the sounds of rigging at night.

he listened to the sea,
gasping into the Gulf of Gaspé,
could not miss the scratch of wind on rope
the sound of cardboard ripping.

once he thought of plates in the cupboard,
remembered scraping noises a file makes over wood,
a lot of creaking in his thorax,
the breathings of a coping saw—

listened until his daughter said it's a
cabinet maker, you got in there.

heartless

there's your double standard,
right there, double bubble heart, the joy
from a child's soapy wand,
fearing someone might in accident
or ancient purpose squash it.

could also have been a pan
filled with water a bottle—
bare to the hot & gritty wind—
could have been a decanter
from which people drank,

in the middle of the floor
        hard and long,
wearing as the Vatican or Vulcan
        himself, the tread hardly worn.
                good on ice, you say,
            spinning every day in sand
            & splattering mud.

            i see, i say,
        i can see it now—
                    it is on its way,
                        it has to
            be this way.

        you have to keep
    your feet, also your eye
            peeled for
    the rainy weather
                in your heart.

perturbations of the heart

sometimes doctors are unable
to find the causes—

the stars in their disasters
call from mid-atlantic,
the waters pouring
wild aneurisms through the heart.

what occurs in certain
zones—do not pretend
you cannot hear them

an "H" in the heart
(after bp nichol)

he was feeling the heat—
a hitch in the gait,
or at any rate,
an itch in the groin.

an H in the heart is what
the poet said it was—
hanging by a thread.

the threat of something,
a dirth of something,
the way we treat one another—
all the disablings and flailings of the heart.

it tears at you, she said,
the too much of it—
too much heat,
too much love,
too much for,
anyone to hear.

Acknowledgements

With thanks to the fine crew at the University of Calgary Press, and particularly to Helen Hajnoczky for her exemplary work as an editor.

In writing this book I have been happily informed by Bill Bryson's wonderful book *A Short History of Nearly Everything*.

Earlier versions of some of these poems have appeared in books (*sunfall, soul searching, passwords*); and in magazines or journals (*border crossings, prairie fire*, and *swift current*).

Photo credit: Jan Horner

dennis cooley has lived his creative life on the prairies, where he
has been a poet, publisher, teacher, critic, theorist, anthologist,
reviewer, organizer, mentor. He was a founding member and three
times president of the Manitoba Writer's Guild, founding editor with
Turnstone Press and professor at St. John's College at the University of
Manitoba.

BRAVE & BRILLIANT SERIES

SERIES EDITOR:

Aritha van Herk, Professor, English, University of Calgary

ISSN 2371-7238 (PRINT) ISSN 2371-7246 (ONLINE)

Brave & Brilliant encompasses fiction, poetry, and everything in between and beyond. Bold and lively, each with its own strong and unique voice, Brave & Brilliant books entertain and engage readers with fresh and energetic approaches to storytelling and verse.

No. 1 · *The Book of Sensations* | Sheri-D Wilson

No. 2 · *Throwing the Diamond Hitch* | Emily Ursuliak

No. 3 · *Fail Safe* | Nikki Sheppy

No. 4 · *Quarry* | Tanis Franco

No. 5 · *Visible Cities* | Kathleen Wall and Veronica Geminder

No. 6 · *The Comedian* | Clem Martini

No. 7 · *The High Line Scavenger Hunt* | Lucas Crawford

No. 8 · *Exhibit* | Paul Zits

No. 9 · *Pugg's Portmanteau* | D. M. Bryan

No. 10 · *Dendrite Balconies* | Sean Braune

No. 11 · *The Red Chesterfield* | Wayne Arthurson

No. 12 · *Air Salt* | Ian Kinney

No. 13 · *Legislating Love* | Play by Natalie Meisner, with Director's Notes
by Jason Mehmel, and Essays by Kevin Allen and Tereasa Maillie

No. 14 · *The Manhattan Project* | Ken Hunt

No. 15 · *Long Division* | Gil McElroy

No. 16 · *Disappearing in Reverse* | Allie McFarland

No. 17 · *Phillis* | Alison Clarke

No. 18 · *DR SAD* | David Bateman

No. 19 · *Unlocking* | Amy LeBlanc

No. 20 · *Spectral Living* | Andrea King

No. 21 · *Happy Sands* | Barb Howard

No. 22 · *In Singing, He Composed a Song* | Jeremy Stewart

No. 23 · *I Wish I Could be Peter Falk* | Paul Zits

No. 24 · *A Kid Called Chatter* | Chris Kelly

No. 25 · *the book of smaller* | rob mclennan

No. 26 · *An Orchid Astronomy* | Tasnuva Hayden

No. 27 · *Not the Apocalypse I Was Hoping For* | Leslie Greentree

No. 28 · *Refugia* | Patrick Horner

No. 29 · *Five Stalks of Grain* | Adrian Lysenko, Illustrated by Ivanka Theodosia Galadza

No. 30 · *body works* | dennis cooley